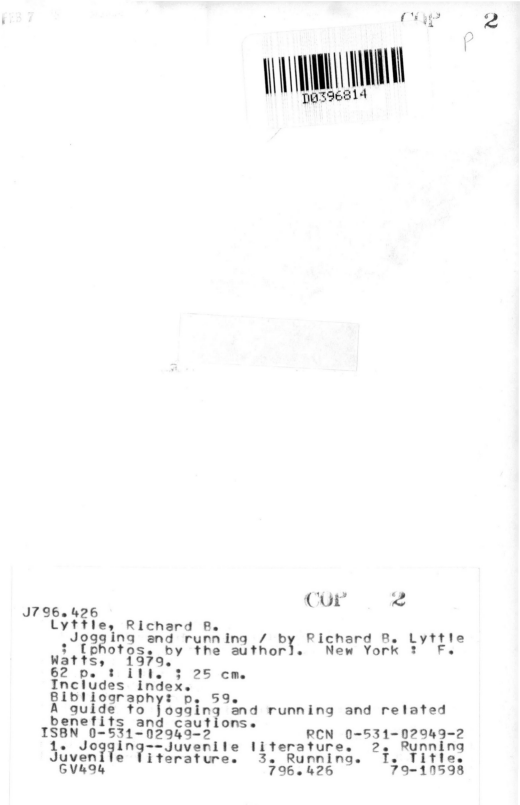

J796.426
   Lyttle, Richard B.
      Jogging and running / by Richard B. Lyttle
   ; [photos. by the author]. New York : F.
   Watts, 1979.
   62 p. : ill. ; 25 cm.
   Includes index.
   Bibliography: p. 59.
   A guide to jogging and running and related
   benefits and cautions.
   ISBN 0-531-02949-2   RCN 0-531-02949-2
      1. Jogging--Juvenile literature. 2. Running
   Juvenile literature. 3. Running. I. Title.
      GV494   796.426   79-10598

General Research Corp.   1979

Jogging and Running

Jogging and Running

BY RICHARD B. LYTTLE

FRANKLIN WATTS

NEW YORK | LONDON | TORONTO | 1979

Photographs by the Author

Library of Congress Cataloging in Publication Data

Lyttle, Richard B
Jogging and running

(A Concise guide)
Bibliography: p.
Includes index.
SUMMARY: A guide to jogging and running and re-
lated benefits and cautions.
1. Jogging—Juvenile literature.   2. Running—Juve-
nile literature.   [1. Jogging.   2. Running]   I. Title.
GV494.L95   796.4′26   79–10598
ISBN 0–531–02949–2

Contents

Acknowledgments

Carrie Chase, Jonathan Becker, Greg Ferrando, Jr.,
Mark Young, and Lisa Divito served as enthusiastic
models for the photos in this book, and their coach,
Jim Patterson, was generous with good advice.
Dr. L. Kent Smith of Boston University Medical Center,
who read the book in manuscript form, made valuable
technical suggestions. Edward F. Dolan, Jr., and
Barthold Fles, two faithful friends, gave steady
encouragement, and Jean, a dear wife, provided the
support and understanding that made the work possible.

To all, my sincere thanks.

This book is for Hilary Sheehan

Jogging and Running

First Steps

By now, it's no secret that running is good for you. It's also one of the least expensive ways to get your body in shape. But above all, running is fun.

Run alone, and you will find freedom from the pressures of a busy life and a crowded world. Run with a group, and you will find new friends. Race, and you will find full satisfaction for a competitive spirit. No wonder running has become one of the most popular activities today. Running is open to all, boys and girls, men and women.

But you undoubtedly have questions, several of them. Finding answers to these questions should be the first step in your venture as a runner.

When should I run? This depends a great deal on your daily schedule, but all you need to benefit from running is a half hour a day, three or four days a week. You should be able to work this time in without great change in your current routine. Some runners rise early and work out before breakfast. Others set aside a half hour at the end of the day. Still others run during their lunch hours. Try to pick a time that is most convenient for you, a time that will make it as easy as possible to start and stick to your running schedule.

Where should I run? A quiet street, a park, the track at a nearby school, an indoor track if one is convenient, a country road: all will serve well for your workouts. In the beginning, you should avoid hills, and experience may tell you that you can't run with comfort on hard surfaces. You may have to restrict your running to grass or a dirt track, but you can almost certainly find the room to run. If you are really stuck, however, talk to joggers who live in your area. Find out where they run. They will undoubtedly be eager to help you.

Should I join a group now? In most cases, no. If you live in a city where it is dangerous to go out alone, however, you should try to find a running partner, preferably someone else who is beginning.

As a beginner, you will want to work on fundamentals. You will be searching for your individual pace and style, and this can be difficult when you run with a group. Also in group running, you are not likely to have much say in deciding when and where you will run. But if you happen to need lots of moral support and encouragement to start a project, a group might help you begin and help you stick to a schedule during the early months.

So the decision to join a group comes down to individual need. Some runners always go out alone. Others must have companionship. Still others compromise. A good compromise might be to solo on weekdays and run with a group on weekends. This lets you work on fundamentals alone during the week and gives you a chance to compare notes with other runners on Saturday or Sunday.

What if I'm sick? The rule is DON'T RUN. If you have a fever, running can expose you to serious heart damage. Even a minor cold presents risks. Certainly, running will not help you get over your cold. Running in poor health simply runs your body down even more. So respect your body and learn to recognize its needs.

What if I'm overweight? Combined with a moderate diet, running will help you lose weight, but make sure first that you really need to lose weight. Weight charts can be misleading because they do not cover body type or growth factors. But if you are sure you have a problem, and if excess pounds limit your physical activity, see a doctor. Tell him or her about your interest in running. In extreme cases, you may have to diet first before you start running, but in most cases, you can start right in running and cutting down on fats and carbohydrates.

Be warned that any crash reducing plan can be dangerous. If you are still growing, a crash plan can stunt your growth. Play it safe. Let a doctor design your diet.

What's the difference between jogging and running? The arbitrary answer is that a jog is anything slower than 8 miles (about 13 km) an hour. A run is anything faster than that pace. There are other differences that you will notice when you start to concentrate on style, but the primary difference is pace. And because pace varies so much with individual effort and ability, I like to refer to any workout as a "run."

How do I get started? This is the big question, and it must be answered in some detail.

Begin slowly and don't begin at all until you have

medical clearance and the right equipment. If you follow these simple rules, you can expect a successful start and a lifetime of happy running.

Medical clearance, if you are in good health and have no special problems, should be a simple matter. If you have been having regular checkups or if you have a family doctor who already knows your medical history, clearance may involve nothing more than a phone call. If your doctor wants to see you before you start, and if he or she recommends an electrocardiogram to check your heart, by all means follow the advice. The doctor's stamp of approval on your running schedule will do great things for your peace of mind, not to mention your continued good health.

You should, of course, check with your doctor if you have a serious weight problem, breathing difficulties, high blood pressure, diabetes, chest pains of any kind, or a family history of heart disease.

Having a special problem does not necessarily mean that you can't run, but it does mean that in addition to clearance, you must have continued medical guidance throughout your running schedule.

Don't get the idea from all this that running will endanger your health. On the contrary, running is now recognized as one of the best things you can do for your body and your mind. Knowing why this is so should help you through any difficulties you may encounter as a beginning runner. So let's examine the health aspects of running.

The Best Exercise

Running will strengthen your heart. If there were no other benefit, a stronger heart would be reason enough to start moving those feet.

The heart acts as a pump. When you increase its efficiency by strengthening its muscles, the heart does not have to work as hard as it did before to do its job. The average adult's pulse rate during normal, slow activity is 70 to 90 beats per minute. The rate of the well-conditioned heart, however, might be somewhere between 40 to 60 beats per minute.

Let's suppose that by strengthening your heart you reduce its rate by 14 beats per minute. Such a reduction is possible with just a few months of regular jogging. It might not sound like much, but look what you will have accomplished. You will have saved your heart 21,000 beats a day, and that works out to 7,300,000 beats a year! Doctors now generally agree that exercise not only helps prevent heart attacks, but it also very probably prolongs life.

The healthy heart thrives on exercise. The same is true of other organs and systems in a healthy body, and because the organs and systems are interrelated, so are the benefits. For instance, by increasing lung capacity with running, you can raise the oxygen content of your blood. With more oxygen in the blood, the burden on your heart can again be lowered. This is why smoking cigarettes, which reduces the blood oxygen, can put a strain on the heart.

The body's circulatory system, which feeds all cells of the body with food and oxygen and draws away cell waste, benefits greatly from exercise. Thus as you improve your circulatory system with exercise, every cell in your body will receive a larger supply of blood and will dispose of wastes more efficiently than ever before. And cells well served by the circulatory system are likely to be healthy cells.

Any exercise, of course, is better than none, but just a few exercises produce lasting benefits to the heart, lungs, and circulatory system.

A "PERFECT" EXERCISE

These beneficial exercises are now called *aerobics*, a word coined by Dr. Kenneth H. Cooper, who pioneered aerobic research when he was a fitness specialist with the United States Air Force.

Measuring such variables as pulse, breathing rate, and particularly oxygen consumption, Dr. Cooper was able to rate the aerobic value of many different exercises. Running and jogging came out at the top of his list. Not only did these activities produce quick benefit, but they also could be followed by almost anyone with just a small sacrifice in time and effort. Three

You don't need a highroad to feel on top
of the world, but a scenic route like this
certainly adds to the joy of running.

to four half-hour workouts a week are all that one needs to achieve and maintain aerobic fitness.

Your ability to see and measure your own progress is perhaps one of the best things about running. Whether you measure your workouts by time or distance or take both time and distance to figure your pace, the progress will be there. After little more than a month, you can look back on your efforts of the first week and find great satisfaction in the strides you have made. Furthermore, you can plan your future development with confidence. Who knows? You may well become more confident about everything you plan in life.

This leads to the mental side of running. Much has been written about the mental well-being and the improvement in attitude, nervous state, and all-around quality of life that comes from regular workouts.

Experiences, of course, differ with each individual, but you can expect changes. Let's face it, sticking to a running routine takes no small measure of discipline. But when you achieve this discipline, when you put yourself in charge of your body, you will receive no small measure of pride.

Shoes

Any runner will tell you that proper running shoes are essential. A good running shoe must be both sturdy and soft, durable and light, flexible and stiff. It is not easy to build all these qualities into a pair of shoes, and this is why shoes will be your major expense as a beginning runner. Fortunately, it need be your only major expense.

Expect to spend a fair amount on your first shoes, and know that you must spend time and care in making your selection. There are scores of brand names to consider. No single brand or model is right for every foot and running style, so don't give too much weight to statements or surveys that put one brand above all others. You want the right shoe for *you*.

Here are some features you should look for in any running shoe:

1. The sole should be made of at least two layers: a soft, inner layer to absorb shock, and a hard outer layer to take wear. The outer layer, usually made of composition rubber, should have a rough surface to assure good grip.

2. The sole should be stiff at the heel and flexible at the toe. You want a firm heel and ankle foundation as well as freedom of motion for the front portion of your foot.

3. The heel of the sole should be a quarter to a half inch (.66 to 1.32 cm) thicker than it is at the toe. This lifts your heels and prevents strain along the back of the legs.

4. Any seams or ribs in the shoe top should be so well-padded that you cannot feel them inside the shoe.

5. The heel area of the shoe top should provide firm support and a tight fit. If the heel counter runs high at the back of the shoe, however, it must be well padded to prevent chafing or cutting.

6. The tongue should be long enough and wide enough to shield the entire lace area of the shoe.

7. The shoe should have a built-in arch support.

Most shoe tops are made of suede, leather, nylon, or a combination of leather and nylon. Many have strengthening strips of leather or plastic. These strips jazz up the appearance of a shoe, but their main purpose should be added support.

IF THE SHOE FITS . . .

After you check all these features in a shoe, the next step is to examine it for fit. The last (inner shape of the sole) should conform to the shape of your foot. It is hard to get a good look at the inner surface of the sole, but the outer contour of the sole provides a good guide to the inner shape.

Some buyers trace their foot and the shoe on a large sheet of paper to compare shape. Another method is to hold the bottom of the right shoe against the bottom of your left foot. This is not an exact test, but it will tell you quickly whether or not a shoe is worth trying on for fit.

When you put the shoe on, make sure that your heel is held firmly in place with no room to slide. Fit along the sides of your foot should be snug but not tight. At the front, the toes should have room to wiggle. The front of the big toe should be a half to three-quarters of an inch (1.32 to 2 cm) back from the end of the last. If the toe comes to or extends beyond the last, the shoe is too small.

When the shoe is laced up, make sure that the pressure along the sides of your foot is even. Now stand up. If the shoe seems to make you lean forward unnaturally, the heel lift is too high for you. If the shoe seems right, however, get the other one on and try jogging down one of the store aisles. Don't let the stares of other customers embarrass you. A few steps of jogging are the best test of all for fit. Walking around simply won't do the trick.

Now what about the arch? This is the trickiest part of the whole fitting process. It's possible that you will find a shoe that fits perfectly in every way except that the arch support does not feel exactly right. Further searching is not likely to solve the problem. If the arch is not too far off, buy the shoes and jog in them a few weeks. Then you will know what is needed to adjust the arch.

Some veteran runners tear out the built-in arch supports and rebuild them with their own padding or a commercial arch support. The Dr. Scholl's supports work well, but you can also use pads of felt or foam rubber. These "cookies" (as they are called) should be bound in place with adhesive tape. If this does not solve the problem, a shoemaker or a foot doctor (podiatrist) can provide a custom-made insert.

After a muddy run, don't try to wet-clean your shoes. Let them dry out slowly, well away from direct heat. Too much heat will harden leather and make it brittle. When the shoes are dry, you can remove the caked mud quickly with a stiff brush.

Finally, heed this warning on running shoes. Don't try to economize. The cheaper models designed to look like running shoes might be all right for casual wear, but they will fall apart in a hurry when you run in them. Tennis shoes also have many drawbacks. They don't absorb moisture, and wet feet combined with the rough, canvas tops lead to blisters. They are also heavy, provide little support, and are poor shock absorbers. Don't run in tennis shoes.

Other Gear

Next in importance after shoes come socks. Sock selection, however, is open to experiment. You can try different styles or combinations until you find what suits you best.

Because good running shoes are well padded, you should not need a thick sock. In fact, some runners wear no socks at all. Most people, however, need socks to assure ventilation and keep feet relatively free of perspiration. A thin cotton sock may be all you need. Avoid pure nylon socks since they don't provide good ventilation. If you are troubled with blisters, try two layers of socks, a thin inner one and a slightly thicker outer one.

Provided your shoes fit, blisters can usually be blamed on excess foot motion within the shoe, moisture from perspiration, or a combination of motion and moisture. The extra thickness of another pair of socks usually solves both problems.

As for the rest of your outfit, just about anything is acceptable. Shorts, an old pair of trousers, a T-shirt, or a sweat shirt, things you undoubtedly already have in your wardrobe, are just fine for the beginner. Be sure, however, not to wear anything so tight or rough that it will bind or chafe. Underwear should be selected with particular care. Men should wear supporters, but this does not necessarily mean an athletic supporter or jockstrap. A pair of cotton jockey shorts is far more comfortable for most runners.

WHAT'S COMFORTABLE FOR YOU
Should women wear bras? Some doctors say a bra is necessary to avoid torn or stretched tissue. Other doctors say there is no danger in running without a bra. To be on the safe side of this debate, your doctor is liable to recommend a bra, and you are liable to end up doing what is most comfortable for you. Many runners compromise with a tight tank top or leotard.

Nipples can become sore on a long run by rubbing against the inside of your shirt. This can happen to both men and women. If you develop this problem put some vaseline on the nipples or protect them with a small bandage.

After you have been jogging a few weeks, you may want to improve your outfit with light-weight shorts and a fancy shirt. For early morning or evening running and for winter workouts, you will want a sweat suit. The cotton outfits are usually unexciting gray,

Wear whatever is comfortable when running, but make sure you're highly visible to oncoming motorists.

and the insides tend to shed when they are new, but they are cheap. If you want one with a hood, expect to pay a little more.

The fancy warm-up suits, available in a multitude of shades and designs, are very comfortable. Most are made of a cotton-nylon combination which assures warmth and good ventilation. A zipper jacket with turtleneck cut provides good body heat control. Expect to pay much more for these, though, than you would for a cotton sweatsuit.

In winter, your hands, head, and ears must be protected. You may also want to wear long underwear. When you are running, however, you usually will have little trouble keeping your body warm. It's the extremities that suffer. (See the chapter on "Other Problems" for tips on winter weather.)

If you jog in the twilight or at night, stick luminous strips on your shoes and the front and back of your shirt so you will be seen in traffic. If storms hit with little warning in your area, carry enough change for a phone call home so that someone can come and rescue you by car. Actually, phone money is a good thing to carry for any emergency.

Finally, include a watch in your gear, preferably a wrist watch. The watch will be your guide during your first workouts.

If you don't have a watch or simply prefer not to wear one when you exercise, you can time your effort by counting the strides of one leg. You should take about 75 strides a minute in a moderate jog. To find your precise pace, jog in place at home in front of a clock for a full minute, counting each time your left foot hits the floor. Then use your total per-minute count as the "timer" for your workouts by counting your strides.

Beginner's Plan

There are two types of beginning runners: those who are out of shape and want to do something to improve, and those who are in good shape and want to do something to stay that way. Within each group, there are a great many levels of fitness. No matter where you stand, you must begin with an experimental frame of mind. This chapter, however, applies almost entirely to runners in the first group: those who are seeking improved fitness. But even if you are already in good shape, reading this chapter will tell you what sort of plan to expect if you ever let yourself get out of shape.

I call this the 20 to 30, hard-easy plan. It borrows heavily from plans recommended by veteran runners and coaches. But it provides greater variation and allows more adjustments than most other plans.

It has these features:

- A 30-minute daily workout with a goal of 20 minutes of jogging or running within each workout.
- Jogging or running time combined with intervals of walking. In other words, a hard-easy plan that allows you to work toward your 20-minute goal with a schedule that best fits your level.
- Great latitude which allows you to experiment, to learn what your body can do, and to find out what progress you can expect.

Despite the latitude, there are some rules you must follow.

Before you start your workout, do some bending exercises to stretch the back of your legs, and begin and end each workout at a walk. Walking is the best exercise to warm up for and warm down after running. (See the chapter on "Runners' Exercises" to find further variations for the warm up and warm down phases of your workouts.)

Work out at least three or four days each week; five days a week if possible. Unless you have been participating in a sport that requires lots of running, do not expect to reach the 20-minute goal in the first or second week. And do not plan your workouts ahead more than a week at a time.

If you wish, you can begin with nothing but walking. Walk at a good pace until you can keep it up without discomfort for 30 minutes. Then you can start to include some jogging.

STARTING SLOWLY

Most beginners want to start jogging right away. But walk first for at least 3 minutes. Then, after you have checked your watch, jog. Don't be too concerned about style at this time. Just try for a smooth, steady pace, and slow again to a walk the moment you begin to tire.

Check your watch. Let's suppose you jogged for 5 minutes. Now keep walking until you feel like jogging again. Once more, clock your jogging time. Keep this up, alternating walking with jogging until you have been out for 25 minutes. Now finish your workout with 5 minutes of walking.

As you walk, you can figure your total jogging time. Suppose you had two stints of 5 minutes each, one of 4 minutes, and one of 3 minutes. That's a total of 17 minutes of jogging. And that's not bad at all.

After you take your shower and change your clothes, you can plan the next workout. Don't try to increase your jogging total immediately. In fact, you can cut back a little if you wish. Suppose on your second day you decide to shoot for 16 minutes. Try to do it in 4 stints of 4 minutes each. This can be your goal for the next several days. Don't try for an increase until you feel like it. Remember, you are still in the experimental phase.

When you decide to increase, you can use one of two methods. You can either add a fifth stint of 4 minutes or you can extend the length of each stint by a minute. Both methods will lead to a total jogging time of 20 minutes—the first goal of your regimen.

Of course, there are many other, more gradual ways to reach the 20-minute goal. And you may find at first that you need long intervals of walking between each jogging stint. But even if you can jog just 10 minutes out of a total 30-minute workout don't be discouraged. You are on your way, and you can look forward to improvement.

VARIETY IS POSSIBLE

The following table showing five typical runners illustrates the variety that is possible with this regimen.

	Start	First Advance	Second Advance	Third Advance
Runner A	3 stints of 4 mins. Total 12	3 stints of 5 mins. Total 15	3 stints of 6 mins. Total 18	3 stints of 7 mins. Total 21
Runner B	3 stints of 3 mins. Total 9	3 stints of 4 mins. Total 12	4 stints of 4 mins. Total 16	5 stints of 4 mins. Total 20
Runner C	2 stints of 7 mins. Total 14	2 stints of 8 mins. Total 16	2 stints of 9 mins. Total 18	2 stints of 10 mins. Total 20
Runner D	4 stints of 3 mins. Total 12	5 stints of 3 mins. Total 15	5 stints of 4 mins. Total 20	
Runner E	4 stints of 4 mins. Total 16	4 stints of 5 mins. Total 20		

In the above examples the first three runners reached or exceeded the 20-minute goal in four stages. The fourth runner did it in three stages by first adding a stint and then lengthening the stints. The fifth runner reached the goal in just two stages by virtue of a strong start.

Your progress may not follow such a simple pattern. For instance, you may have trouble at first running stints of equal time. You may tail off, running 6 minutes your first stint, 4 your second, and just 1 in your final effort. Your first challenge should be balancing your regimen into jogging stints of equal time.

Slow your pace, shorten your first stint, or combine both slower pace and a shorter first stint. Working toward balance will teach you quickly how to judge your ability.

With a balanced regimen, you will be better able to advance smoothly toward your goal. And with steady work, you will be amazed at how quickly you can advance.

Sometimes, progress seems to come overnight. This is why it is important that you not plan your regimen more than a week ahead. As those days come when you feel you can do more, you should be ready to lengthen your stints or do more of them. You should not be locked into a schedule that will hold you back.

Most beginners advance by a series of plateaus. For ten days, for instance, you may seem to be capable of no more than 4 minutes of jogging at a time. Then, you will suddenly find that you can jog for 6 or 7 minutes with ease. Adjust your regimen to fit this improvement at once.

After you reach your total of 20 minutes of jogging, your next goal will be to cut back on your walking intervals. Eventually, you will want to jog steadily for 20 minutes with the only walking coming at the beginning and the end of your workout.

At this stage you will have reached the level where that second group of beginners (those who take up jogging to maintain fitness) start their regimens. You can now consider new goals: longer workouts, pace, and specific distances.

Meanwhile, there is something else that you should begin to concentrate on. For your first few days you should not worry about style. By now, however, it should be receiving your full attention.

Style

Relax!

There it is. One word of advice that is more important than anything else that can be said to beginners. If you run with tension, you will tire quickly, you are almost sure to experience pain, and you will not be able to develop your own style.

Don't worry about how you look to others. Don't think about how fast or how slow you go. Don't stare down at your feet. Relax!

Unfortunately, the more you are told about style, the more you think about it, and the more you think about it, the more you are liable to tense up.

Don't think about it constantly, but when you do think about it, consider just one point at a time. This way you can pick up faults and correct them as you go on your way to developing a style that is right for you.

The most common fault among beginners is tension in the upper body, particularly the shoulders and the neck. This quickly leads to an aching back. Back and shoulder ache can also be caused by tension in the arms.

Hold your head up in a comfortable position. A slight forward lean is normal, but this lean should be from the hips up. Your trunk, neck, and head should be pretty much in line.

Bend your elbows so that your forearms ride freely between your hips and the bottom of your rib cage with a natural swing. Your left arm should move forward with your right leg; your right arm with your left leg. Clenched fists or rigidly locked elbows will restrict this natural balancing motion of arms and legs. Flopping elbows or wrists will produce a sloppy, uneven gait.

To show yourself how closely your arm and leg motion are linked, experiment as you jog by consciously forcing your arms to move faster. Your legs will move faster automatically.

Incidentally, when many runners break from a jog into a running stride, the arm motion slows. This is because with the longer stride of running, foot pace actually slows. You don't need as many steps to cover the same distance. You can experiment with this, too, and perhaps discover your personal dividing line between jogging and running.

BREATHING

Breathe with an open mouth. You will not take in enough air with nose breathing alone. And breathe with your rib cage and your diaphragm, the flat muscle that separates your lungs from your stomach. When you expand your diaphragm, your stomach area expands a bit. If you breathe with both chest and stomach, you will be using all available muscles for efficient breathing.

You may be tempted to fix breathing rate with foot cadence. For instance, you might want to breathe in with every other strike of your right foot. There is no harm in this at first, but don't let it become a habit. With training, you will be able to take slower, deeper breaths.

Talking is a good test for breathing rate. If you can't talk in a normal voice, you are working too hard and breathing too fast. Slow your pace. Breathing faster than you have to brings on hyperventilation, a condition that changes the oxygen-carbon dioxide balance in your blood. This can lead to dizziness. If you can pass the talking test, however, there is very little danger of hyperventilation.

Your legs should swing from the hips, moving in line with your direction of travel. This advice sounds almost too obvious to mention, but it is surprising how many beginners let their legs and feet wander from the true course. For some reason, women seem to have more difficulty with this problem than men.

SHUFFLING AND OVER-STRIDING

Shuffling and over-striding are two other leg motion defects. Shuffling occurs because you do not lift your thighs high enough. When your knees straighten to bring your feet forward, your feet scrape the ground. This is hard on shoes, hard on your legs, and it invites tripping. Shuffling can usually be cured with just a little conscious effort. If it persists, include jogging in place with waist-high thigh lifts in your warm-up exer-

Greg shows good style. Notice that he leans slightly forward from the hips.

cises. Of course, if you start shuffling because of fatigue, stop running and finish your workout at a walk.

Over-striding is usually due to a conscious, abnormal effort to cover more ground with each step than is natural for your pace or your build. It is another defect that will vanish if you relax. As your pace picks up, the length of your stride should increase naturally, but forcing a longer stride with no change of pace does nothing to improve your performance. On the contrary, it will put such a heavy strain on your leg muscles that you will soon have to cut back both your stride and your pace.

FOOT STRIKE

Foot strike, how the sole of your shoe meets the ground, is probably the most discussed phase of style. Beginners seem to be most comfortable using a flat-footed strike with the heel and toe areas meeting the ground simultaneously. As you travel forward over the foot, the heel lifts and you push off with the toes.

With another style called heel strike, the toe area does not touch the ground until forward motion rocks the foot forward. Flat-footed strike and heel strike are the two most popular styles, but it would be wrong to claim that one is better than the other. However, some runners, particularly those with a slight tendency to over-stride, develop sore heels or ankles with a heel strike. Changing to a flat-footed style usually cures the soreness as well as the over-striding tendency.

Toe strike is the least common style. Here the toe area meets the ground first. The heel drops momentarily as you travel forward, but it lifts again as you push off on your toes. It seems like wasted motion, and it probably is, but a few runners can't seem to adjust to any other style.

Running coaches say that sprinters must stay on their toes, but that distance runners should use the flat-footed strike or the heel strike. Experience seems to support this advice. The joggers and runners I know who began with a toe strike gave up the style as soon as they took up long distance workouts.

Bounce, with too much up and down motion of the entire body, is also a waste of energy and likely to produce sore feet and joints. Concentrate on gliding forward with each step. Sometimes bounce is caused by too much arm motion, arm tension, or a tendency to lift the hands too high with each stride. Some people tend to run with their hands up at shoulder level. They should be kept down, even with your waist.

If you run with a group, you and your friends can check each other's style. Better yet, if you know a veteran runner, ask him or her to watch you run. The veteran will be a willing critic and is almost sure to pick up subtle defects you or your friends might never notice.

If you run alone, you can sometimes see faults by watching your shadow when it falls to one side and slightly ahead of you. The shadow will not show much detail, but it will tell you if you are running with a smooth rhythm.

Many solo runners make a habit of checking style just two or three times during a workout. They don't think about it until after they have been moving along as relaxed as possible for at least 5 minutes. Then they ask themselves some specific questions.

You might ask yourself, for instance, if your legs are tracking in line with your line of travel. If they are

not, concentrate on correcting the defect. How about your hands? Are they clenched? Are they too high? Are they flopping like bird wings?

Are you looking straight ahead? Is your head up in a normal position? Some people have a tendency to lower their heads and run like charging billy goats. This invites a stiff neck.

After several workouts with spot checks on style, you should be able to recognize one or two specific faults. Then, your style checks will become easier. Just look for these faults. It may simply be a matter of un-clenching your hands or lifting your head.

Then you can move on, free and easy and *relaxed.*

**From the front you can see
that Greg keeps his elbows
close to his body and that
his feet track perfectly.
There is no wasted motion.**

New Challenges

Perhaps it took you two months, perhaps just two weeks, or maybe you were one of those well-conditioned beginners who could start right out with twenty minutes of steady jogging. Whatever your experience was, you are now ready for new challenges.

There are many ways to add challenge to your regimen. If you have a schedule that limits your workouts to a half hour, you can increase your effort by increasing your pace. Include some running. Use the same hard-easy approach by alternating stints of running with stints of jogging.

To break into a run, increase the push-off with the toe of your back foot and extend your stride. Be careful to avoid tension. Clenching your fists or thrusting your head forward will restrict rather than ease your progress.

Your foot strike may change. In jogging, your front foot is planted either directly below or slightly ahead of a vertical line from the knee. In running, with the extended stride, your foot will be planted well ahead of this knee line. As a consequence, you may change from a flat-footed strike to a heel strike.

If this proves uncomfortable, shorten your running stride a little so that you can continue using the flat-footed style.

You may begin with just two or three short stints of running in your daily workout, but as you progress you can extend these stints until you are running half or even full time.

Another way to add challenge, if your schedule allows it, is to simply extend the time of your workout. Build up gradually to 25, then 30 minutes of jogging. It is possible, of course, to change your pace as well, working short stints of running into your longer workouts.

Many runners with limited time during the week schedule a long workout on the weekend. This provides variety as well as a new challenge. If it's possible to work in one long workout during the week as well, so much the better. Two long workouts alternated with two short ones during the week is another application of the hard-easy approach.

DISTANCE

Distance can provide another challenge. You may have already figured out the distances covered in your workouts even though I suggested that you measure your first efforts by time alone. The problem with using both time and distance in describing a beginner's program is that it tends to bring out competitive urges. Trying to see how fast you can cover a measured distance, running against the clock rather than with it, risks over-extension.

Clocking runs over a known distance is fine for race training, but for recreational or fitness runners, distance should be simply an alternate way of measuring effort.

If you run on a track, it is easy to figure distance as long as you know the length of the lap. Most school tracks are designed with quarter-mile (.40 km) laps. Four times around equals one mile (1.61 km).

Tracks have the advantage of soft surface: Tartan, cinder, or dirt; but if you use a track, change directions from time to time so that you do not get locked into turning just one way in all your workouts.

If you run along a roadside, you can measure off distances with a car's odometer, but this is not possible when you run in parks or over cross-country trails. You can still get a good idea of distance on such trails by timing yourself on a measured course such as a track, and then timing yourself at the same pace over the trail. If you run an 8-minute mile (1.61 km) on the track, and it takes you 24 minutes to run your trail, then you can figure the trail route is about 3 miles (4.83 km) long.

Most veteran runners measure their effort by distance rather than time. In conversation, it certainly sounds more impressive to speak of your miles or kilometers than minutes. But no matter how you measure workouts, stick with the hard-easy approach.

Moving from a jog to a run, Carrie extends her leg and arm motion as she opens her pace. The right leg has just pushed off, and is about to swing forward in a long stride.

You can use your long days to start working toward your maximum level of effort. Everyone has a maximum—6 miles (about 10 km), 10 (16 km), perhaps 15 (25 km). It is that point where you have had enough, where endurance gives out. You no longer can hold your pace, and further effort produces no benefit and might even be harmful.

Of course, if you are still growing or if your condition is still improving, your maximum will slowly improve, but don't push it too hard. Working to or close to your maximum once or twice a month will tell you what new challenges your future may hold.

THE PULSE TEST

If working toward a maximum does not appeal to you, then you should make a practice of taking the pulse tests. Doctors have found that benefit from exercise, what Dr. Cooper calls the "training effect," can be achieved only if you boost your heart rate to 70 per cent of its maximum.

The maximum heart rate varies with age. To figure your maximum, subtract your age from 220. If you are ten, your maximum will be 210. If you are fifteen, your maximum will be 205. Thus, training effect for the ten-year-old will be achieved with a pulse of 147 beats per minute (70 per cent of 210). For the fifteen-year-old, training effect will be achieved with a pulse of 143.5 (70 per cent of 205).

Take your pulse when you start your warm down walk at the end of your workout. A simple method is to measure your pulse for 10 seconds and then multiply the count by six to figure the total beats per minute. If your pulse is 10 per cent or more lower than it should be, you should increase your effort either by picking up your pace or giving more time to your work-outs.

THE 12-MINUTE TEST

Yet another way to evaluate your progress is the 12-minute test. Devised by Dr. Cooper, the test relates fitness to the distance you can cover in 12 minutes of jogging or running.

Dr. Cooper rates performance by sex and age level. The following scores are for novice men and women under thirty years of age.

Very Poor—less than a mile (1.61 km) for men and less than .95 of a mile (1.53 km) for women.

Poor—from 1 to 1.24 miles (1.61 to 2 km) for men and from .95 to 1.14 miles (1.53 to 1.84 km) for women.

Fair—from 1.25 to 1.49 miles (2 to 2.40 km) for men and from 1.15 to 1.34 miles (1.84 to 2.16 km) for women.

Good—from 1.50 to 1.74 miles (2.41 to 2.80 km) for men and from 1.35 to 1.64 miles (2.17 to 2.64 km) for women.

Excellent—1.75 miles (2.82 km) or more for men and 1.65 miles (2.66 km) or more for women.

At first glance, these figures look arbitrary, but they are based on hundreds of tests with complicated instruments that measure oxygen intake, blood absorption of oxygen, and efficiency of the circulatory system.

Dr. Cooper does not recommend the test for beginners, and I suggest if you start taking the test once or twice a year or perhaps as often as once a month that you use it as a tool to measure progress only. Don't let a poor rating discourage you or an excellent rating make you complacent. The test does not measure potential, nor does it take into account the rapid changes and ranges of abilities found during the growing years.

Running and Growth

For years, with no scientific knowledge to guide them, coaches and parents told young would-be runners to *wait*.

"Wait until you're a little older."

"Wait until you have some meat on your bones."

"Wait."

It was discouraging, but the picture is gradually changing. With the thunder of running feet increasing all across the country, children simply refused to wait. They wanted to be part of the running movement. So they ran, and their parents and their coaches were surprised time and again to see that no apparent harm was being done.

Today, the national clubs and organizations are having a hard time scheduling enough age group races at all distances to keep up with the demand. Five-year-olds have even run marathons.

Obviously, "wait" is no longer the byword.

There is, however, still good reason for caution. For one thing, the research is still in progress. The reports are not final. Second, the studies so far show that children have strengths and weaknesses quite different from those of adults. Because it's smaller, a child's heart must pump faster than an adult's heart. Also, a child's blood does not have the oxygen-carrying capacity of adult blood.

This affects performance in any running event that creates oxygen debt, the condition in which the body is burning up more oxygen than the lungs and heart can supply. Fully grown athletes in many track and field events train to increase their ability to handle oxygen debt, and they can handle it for short periods. Children cannot handle it.

In addition to the oxygen problem, children do not have the muscle development or strength for speed running. Thus they should avoid any speed running of 100 yards (91.44 m) or more that will produce oxygen debt or strain.

Children, however, do have a high rate of oxygen intake and this gives them remarkable endurance. It didn't take a lot of sophisticated research to make this discovery. All you have to do is watch children at play. In an hour they can cover 2 miles (3.22 km) or more with stop and go running, and they seem capable of playing this way for hours on end.

So, contrary to tradition, it appears that children should be encouraged to take long, slow runs, and that they should not participate in the short, so-called easy races that have long been part of their school activities. Dr. Ernst van Aaken, a German coach and physician and a pioneer in the recent research, concludes that children were made for moderate endurance running. New Zealand's Arthur Lydiard agrees.

When children reach puberty, however, complexities cloud the picture. So many body changes occur, and the rate of change varies so much among individuals, that it is difficult to make any generalities.

As you might suspect, the experts continue to be cautious in drawing any conclusions about strenuous exercise during the years of puberty. What it boils down to is that you, too, should be cautious. Continue running, but be ready to adjust your regimen to fit the demands and limitations of your changing body.

Your skeletal growth will be rapid. You might shoot up 2 or 3 inches (about 5 to 7.5 cm) in less than a year. Your muscular strength may triple in four or five years. Your body chemistry will change, and this will bring changes in your appetite and your need for sleep.

There will certainly be days when you don't feel like running. All you may want to do is rest. If this happens, take some time off. Start running again when you feel up to it.

You may experience growing pains in joints and muscles. Such pains are no joke. Nurse them the same way you would nurse an injury. Shin splints, a common teen-age complaint, may force you to alter your program. (See the Chapter on "Aches and Pains.")

Through it all, you will see gradual improvement in your physical ability. In just a few years of change, your speed will increase. Indeed, if you participate in high school track, you may discover that you have potential as a sprinter. But don't force your development. Be patient, and remember that your best years, from ages twenty to thirty, are the years when you can expect top performance in many sports. Don't jeopardize that performance now by putting too much strain on your growing body.

Runners' Exercises

Walking at the beginning and end of your workouts is usually adequate in your first days' running. But before long you will begin searching for other exercises, both to add variety and to guard against stiff and sore muscles that you may experience when you take on new challenges.

Don't replace walking with other exercises. Walking to warm up and warm down is necessary to keep from putting a strain on your heart that sudden changes in demand can make. Walking also gives the leg muscles a good stretch which is particularly important for warming up.

S-T-R-E-T-C-H
To get added muscle stretch, simple bend overs are hard to beat. They not only stretch the muscles in the back of the legs, but they also give the spine good extension, and this promotes relaxed running.

You don't have to touch your toes with your finger tips. Just bend at the waist, relaxing so the weight of your head, arms, and trunk carries you down. If you don't bend your knees, the muscles from your buttocks to your achilles tendon will receive full benefit of the exercise. Don't bob up and down or use jerking motions. You want a slow, smooth stretch.

Yoga exercises are popular with runners because they are all done slowly and smoothly. Try this yoga version of the bend over: Stand with your feet together and your legs straight. Now bend at the waist and bring your arms down so that you can clasp your hands behind your legs. Gradually lower your clasped hands, sliding them down to your calves and on toward your ankles. When you reach the lowest point possible, pull with your arms and hold your position for a count of ten before straightening up slowly. Repeat this exercise two or three times before each workout. You will soon be delighted with your new-found flexibility.

Yoga leg pulls provide even greater stretching force. Sit on the floor with your left leg extended and your right leg bent at the knee so that your heel is tucked into your crotch. Keep the bent knee pressed to the floor. Now bend forward, extending your arms so that you can grip the calf of your extended leg with both hands. Pull by cocking your elbows outward. The force should bring your face close to your knee. Hold this position for a count of ten. Then repeat the exercise at least once more before changing positions to stretch the other leg.

If tight calf muscles and achilles tendons make bending exercises and leg pulls difficult for you, try wall push-ups. Stand with feet together about arm's length away from the wall. Keeping your body straight,

Left: the yoga bend will quickly increase your flexibility. Carrie, who already has good flexibility, holds the position for a count of ten. Above: with the yoga leg pull, you exert a powerful stretching force on your leg muscles. You can build this force gradually as flexibility improves.

lean forward, bracing your palms on the wall at shoulder height. Keep both heels on the floor as you increase your lean by cocking your elbows. Lean as far as you can without lifting your heels. Then push away and repeat slowly six times. When you can touch your forehead to the wall, you should have enough flexibility to move on to regular bends or leg pulls.

STRENGTH

All the exercises listed so far have been muscle stretchers, but there are two muscle strengthening exercises runners should consider. One of them, the sit-up exercise, is highly recommended for everyone. The other, the toe-lift exercise, is for runners with weak ankles.

Why are sit-ups so important? Running does very little to strengthen the abdominal muscles. These are the muscles that support many vital internal organs. Good tone in these muscles prevents a pot belly and guards against discomfort and illness.

Try to do sit-ups with your knees bent, your feet flat on the floor, and your hands clasped behind your neck. You may have to brace your feet under a heavy piece of furniture. Come all the way up with your face close to your knees and let yourself down slowly. Try to build up to 20 repetitions daily. If you can't do sit-ups from this position, start doing them with your hands at your sides.

Doctors often recommend sit-ups for back problems, and this is a clue to runners who develop sore backs. Running will strengthen back muscles, but when the back strengthens without a corresponding increase in the strength of the abdominal muscles, there is an imbalance of forces which causes the back muscles to stiffen, sometimes with painful spasms.

Weak ankle muscles can be strengthened with a regular routine of toe-lifts. Use a stack of magazines or a board about 2 inches (5 cm) thick for a platform. Stand with the balls of your feet on this platform and your heels on the floor. Now lift yourself slowly up and down on your toes, letting your heels sink to the floor with each repetition.

Strengthening exercises can be done at any time. They need not be part of your warm up, but you must do the exercises regularly to gain full benefit from them.

When you warm down, the important thing is to keep moving by walking or some other activity for at least 5 minutes after the heavy phase of your workout. Never lie down or flop into a chair while your heart is still beating fast. To work out stiffness, you can swing your arms, rock your shoulders up and down, or roll your neck as you walk. Experience will soon tell you when your heart rate has eased off enough to do some yoga exercises or head for the shower. If you are not certain at first, however, check your pulse. If it is 120 beats per minute or more, keep moving until it drops below 120.

As you continue running, you will undoubtedly develop a preference for some exercises and a curiosity about others. Experiment with new exercises. Be ready to add variety. The warm up and warm down phases of your workout should provide just as much pleasure and satisfaction as your running.

Aches and Pains

If you do not overextend yourself; if you stretch before and after running; if you wear well-padded shoes of good fit; and if you avoid obvious hazards such as icy streets or heavy traffic, injuries should be the least of your problems.

Strangely enough, however, injuries are a leading topic of conversation in running circles, particularly if there are racing buffs around. So let's discuss some of the typical aches and pains and their cures. They might never concern you, but at least you will know what your fellow runners are talking about.

Blisters, calluses, tennis toe, and sore arches and heels can often be blamed on shoes of poor fit, but don't be too quick to blame your running shoes. Your everyday shoes may be causing stress or irritation that does not bother you until you start to run. Some women torture their toes, arches, and heels for the sake of fashion. Be kind to your feet at all times.

The causes of blisters have already been described, but if blisters persist or turn into calluses and you are sure that shoe fit cannot be improved, your next step should be to consult a podiatrist, preferably one who specializes in sports. He or she may be able to design a shoe insert or alter the shoe itself to relieve pressure on the trouble spot.

To treat a blister, puncture it near the lower edge with a sterile needle and squeeze out the moisture. Before you put shoes on again, cover the spot with a bandage to prevent further irritation.

If you have a callus, soak your foot in warm water for several minutes. Then reduce the hard area by rubbing it gently with a pumice stone. Sore arches or sore heels can often be cured with arch supports or heel cups. (Heel cups can be purchased in most sports shops.) But, again, if these devices don't relieve the problem, consult a doctor.

Tennis or runner's toe, which is a blood blister under the nail, looks terrible and can sometimes be painful. The cause is toe crowding. You may need shoes of looser fit, but if you don't want to give up on your present shoes, try cutting two slits in the top of the toe area. Don't cut through the lining, and keep the slits small, no more than a half to three-quarters of an inch (or about 1.5 to 2 cm) long. In bad cases of runner's toe, the nail will eventually drop off. You will grow a new one, and if you have relieved the pressure, the nail will be perfectly healthy.

MORTON'S FOOT

If you have the condition known as Morton's foot (the second toe longer than the big toe) you may have any one of a number of problems. Sore feet, ankles, knees, and even a painful pinch of the sciatic nerve, which runs through the pelvis and into the thigh, have all been traced to Morton's foot.

When you run, the leading toe receives the most pressure. The big toe of a normal foot can take this pressure, but the second toe often cannot. Soreness in the toes and the ball of the foot is usually the first symptom. But runners who try to compensate by flexing the toes or changing their running style to shift pressure to the big toe often experience pain in leg joints.

You can see if you have Morton's foot simply by looking at your bare feet. The condition does not always cause trouble, but if it starts giving you any pain at all, check with a doctor. In most cases an insert that shifts pressure to your big toe will solve the problem.

SPRAINS AND STRAINS

Mildly aching ankles are a common complaint among beginners, but if pain persists it could be due to too much work on hard surfaces or else one of the foot problems described above. Ankle sprains, caused by a misstep or fall, should have a doctor's prompt attention. Running will strengthen ankles so that soreness usually goes away with time, and the risk of sprain is greatly reduced.

A swollen achilles tendon (a condition known as tendonitis) can be very painful. Too much running, too little warm up, or trying to compensate for a foot problem are common causes of the inflammation, but shoes with low heels might also be the fault. Inserts that lift the heel or simply a slower pace will usually cure tendonitis.

Sore calves, like sore ankles, are a common beginner's complaint. Again, a temporary reduction in running time or a slower pace will usually relieve the problem. Shin splints (pain along the length of the shins—rarely serious but often painful) are caused by overwork, too fast a pace, or running on hard surfaces. Running in shoes with poorly cushioned soles will also bring on pain in the tissues covering the shins.

Chronic knee pain should have medical attention. It could be that the cartilage between your kneecap and the joint socket is torn or bruised. If this cartilage slips out of place, the pain and stiffness will put you out of action. So don't take chances with a bad knee. Mild knee aches may be due again to overwork or hard surfaces. Cut back on your schedule, but if the ache persists, see a doctor.

A stiff or sore back after running can often be cured by increasing back stretching exercises in the warm up and warm down phases of your workout. And as already mentioned, the problem might be due to weak abdominal muscles. Persistent back pain, like chronic knee pain, should have a doctor's attention.

Other Problems

Bad weather, which includes very hot days as well as stormy days, can be a problem if you don't respect it.

Rather than take a chance with extremes in weather, it is safer and much more comfortable to stay inside and get your daily workout by jogging in place, using a jump rope, or pumping the wheel of an exercise bicycle.

Of course, if you have access to an indoor track, you can go right on with your running schedule with no weather worries. And if you are hardy, you can go out and run in rain or snow. But don't be *fool*hardy.

Slippery mud or leaves, ice, cold winds, and conditions that make it difficult for you to see or be seen are all serious hazards. Cold weather alone, however, need not keep you inside provided you dress warmly, taking particular care to protect your hands and ears. Wear good mittens and ear muffs or a pull-down, knitted cap. Some runners wear ski masks.

With proper protection, you may find that cold, clear days suit you perfectly. But beware of wind in freezing weather. Wind carries off body heat quickly, so it's best to stay inside on freezing, windy days.

Hot, humid weather poses another problem: heatstroke. Sometimes fatal, heatstroke is due to dehydration. When the body's water supply falls too low to keep your natural cooling system functioning, your temperature will climb rapidly to the danger level, sometimes several degrees above normal. Death from heatstroke is usually caused by heart stoppage brought on by the extreme body temperature.

Fortunately, there are usually plenty of early warning symptoms: thirst, dry skin, weakness, and dizziness. If you run in hot weather, drink lots of water before and after, and stop running at once at the first sign of discomfort. Cool off in the shade, then head slowly for the nearest water. A cold bath, even an ice bath, anything that will cool the body is the standard treatment for advanced heatstroke.

DOGS

Dogs can be a real annoyance, particularly in rural or suburban areas where they are allowed to run free. Even some city parks have dog problems. One trick that usually works when a dog comes barking at your heels is to stop, face the dog, and pretend to pick up a rock. Most dogs turn tail at this. But if you have a problem dog on your route, your only solution may be to change routes. Unfortunately, most dog owners, when and if they can be located, are rarely sympathetic enough with your problem to take corrective measures. And unless you are actually bitten, there are too few effective and legal steps you can take to force a solution.

Runners must obey all the rules of traffic, both for their own safety and the safety of others. When there are no walk ways, run on the left side of a roadway. Don't run through red lights, and if you go out with a group, don't bunch up so that you obstruct car or pedestrian traffic.

Visibility is the key to safe running. Cars coming out of alleys or around blind turns are serious hazards. Obviously, a driver who can't see you can't avoid you.

If you must run in the dark, pick your routes with care. Even if you wear reflective tape on your shoes and your clothing, it will not help you much in congested traffic.

HILLS

Hills are more of a challenge than a problem. The trick is to shorten your stride going up and coming down the slopes. Don't try for any speed records.

Going up hill, even with a high knee lift, your stride may be no more than 10 to 12 inches (about 25 to 30 cm). A slight side to side sway of your shoulders and upper body may help you work up the hills.

Coming down a slope, you may be tempted to open up with a long stride. You might go fast, but you will have little control and the jarring foot strike of fast downhill running will produce sore joints in a hurry. So come down with a short, controlled stride. Don't risk a spill.

As a rule, you should work into hill running gradually. Too much uphill work will cause sore calves or tendonitis. Too much downhill work, even with short strides, can cause sore heels, ankles, knees, or shin splints.

Racing

Is competitive running for you?

The best way to answer this question is to try racing. You may have already started to think about entering a race. In fact, you may have started running with the hope of going into competition.

Racing is a wonderful test of ability. Just finishing some of the endurance runs will give you a fine sense of accomplishment. And there are social benefits. When you take up racing, you will join men and women who are held together by a strong bond. You are almost sure to learn from these people.

It must be stressed, however, that racing is not for everyone. Competition with its hard training and its pressure requires unusual dedication and a special personality.

Usually, you can find out if you are suited for competition by entering a race for fun. These are casual events sponsored by local running clubs. There are no entry restrictions or fees and no prizes.

If your first race sparks your interest, then you can begin planning a future in serious competition.

One of the first decisions you may face at this stage is picking your event. Are you an endurance runner, capable of long distances? Or are you a fast pacer, more suited for shorter runs?

In racing circles, events of 6 miles (about 10 km) or less are considered short runs. Anything longer than that is an endurance run.

The best known events in the first category are the mile (1.61 km) and the 1,500 meter race. The best known in the second category, of course, is the marathon—26 miles and 385 yards (42.20 km).

Taking Dr. Cooper's 12-minute test may help you select your event. If you score at the excellent level, you probably have enough speed for the shorter races. If the best you can score is a good rating, however, then you probably should concentrate on the endurance runs.

Incidentally, women, who have a higher percentage of fatty tissue on their bodies than men, do well in endurance runs because they can store a greater reserve of energy. Men, who have a higher percentage of muscle than women, tend to excel at the shorter, faster runs.

If you plan to race in school competition, the decision on your event may be made by your coach or

Is competitive running for you? Informal races should give you the answer. A school race or one sponsored by a local club gives the right informal atmosphere.

by the school agenda. Junior highs usually do not stage any races longer than a mile (1.61 km). Your high school, however, will almost certainly have a cross-country team, with events of 6 to 10 miles (about 10 to 16 km) or more.

If school agendas are limited, you can still find serious racing in events sanctioned by the Road Runners Club, the Amateur Athletic Union, or some other national or international organization.

School competition has the advantage of good coaching. If you enter races outside the school, however, you will most likely be your own coach and trainer.

There are many theories about training, but the foundation for all work, whether you plan on short runs or long ones is endurance. True, pace is very important for the short runs, but if you lack the endurance to hold your pace, you will have little success.

You build endurance by long, daily workouts. The workouts might include trial runs of the race you plan to enter. Speed runners make great use of trial runs in order to find their best pace. Endurance runners, however, do not include many trials. A marathon runner will rarely train by running a marathon. The marathoner may cover 50 or more miles (80 or more km) a week, but not 26 miles (about 42 km) in a single workout. That would be so exhausting that it would interrupt the daily training schedule.

An adult who has been running regularly for recreation will usually need at least three months of hard training to prepare for serious competition. Youngsters often do not take as long. In all cases, sensible habits during training are vital. Eat balanced meals and get plenty of sleep.

Some distance racers practice carbohydrate loading, a system of limiting and then increasing carbohydrate intake during the week before a race. Don't get into this until you have full growth and enough experience to know your body's needs and capabilities in racing conditions. The most important rule on diet is to avoid a big meal before a race. Some racers take nothing but fruit juice on race day.

In your first race, don't hurt your effort with too fast a start. This is the most common error of beginning racers. They may have trained well. They may know their right pace exactly, but in the excitement of the start, they jump out like sprinters. Long before the finish, they have burned up so much energy that they can do little more than shuffle.

Don't be too dismayed if this happens to you in your first race, but do learn from the experience. It would be highly unusual to win your early races against experienced runners. As a beginner, your most important goal will be to finish the race in good condition and good form.

As a final word, don't ever let the competitive spirit influence your good judgment. If you become exhausted, feel dizzy, or experience any other kind of serious discomfort, walk for a while or drop out. It's no disgrace.

Remember, there will always be other races.

For More Information

Write to:

Amateur Athletic Union of the United States
3400 W. 86th Street
Indianapolis, Indiana 46268

Road Runners Club of America
3115 Whispering Pines
Silver Spring, Maryland 20906

For Further Reading

Batten, Jack. *The Complete Jogger.* New York: Harcourt Brace Jovanovich, 1977.

Bowerman, William J., and Harris, W.E. *Jogging.* New York: Grosset and Dunlap, 1967

Cooper, Kenneth H. *Aerobics.* New York: Bantam Books, 1968.

———. *The New Aerobics.* New York: Bantam Books, 1970.

Fixx, James F. *The Complete Book of Running.* New York: Random House, 1977.

Lance, Kathryn. *Running for Health and Beauty: A Complete Guide for Women.* Indianapolis and New York: Bobbs-Merrill Co., 1977.

Lyttle, Richard B. *The Complete Beginner's Guide to Physical Fitness.* Garden City, N.Y.: Doubleday and Co., 1978.

Runner's World, eds. *The Young Runner.* Mountain View, Calif.: World Publications, 1973.

Index

Racing, 33, 53–54, 56–57
Reflective tape, 16, 52
Relaxation, 22, 26, 27, 29, 40
Road Runners Club, 56, 58
Runner's toe, 47
Running gear, 13–14, 16, 50
Running surfaces, 2, 33

Schedules, 1–2
Sciatic nerve, 47–48
Shin splints, 39, 49, 52
Shoes, 9–13, 16, 24, 46–49
Shuffling, 24, 26
Sit-ups, 44
Sleep, 39, 56
Socks, 13
Speed running, 38, 39, 54, 56
Sprains, 48
Sprinters, 27, 39
Strength, 38, 39
Strengthening exercises, 44–45
Stretching exercises, 40–41, 44,
  46, 49
Stride, 16, 26, 30, 31, 52
Style, 21–24, 26–27, 29, 48
Supporters, 14
Sweatsuits, 14, 16

Talking, 24

Tendonitis, 48, 52
Tennis shoes, 12
Tennis toe, 46, 47
Tension, 22–23, 27, 30
Timing, 16
Toe-lifts, 44, 45
Toes, 47, 48
Tracks, 33, 50
Traffic, 46, 52
Training, 53, 56, 57
Training effect, 34
12-minute test, 35–36, 54
20 to 30 plan, 17–21

Underwear, 14, 16
Upper body, 22–23

Walking, 18, 19, 21, 40, 45
Wall push-ups, 41, 44
Warm-down, 18, 34, 40, 45, 49
Warm-up, 18, 24, 40, 45, 49
Warm-up suits, 16
Watches, 16, 18, 19
Weather, 50–51
Weight loss, 3
Winter running, 14–16, 50–51
Women, 14, 24, 46, 54

Yoga exercises, 41, 45